Copyright © 1996 by Francis Lincoln Limited

For photographic acknowledgements and copyright details,
see pages 84-91.

First published as A Treasury of Prayers
in Great Britain in 1996 by Francis Lincoln Limited,
4 Torriano Mews, Torriano Avenue, London NW5 2RZ

Edited by Rev. Victor Hoagland, C. P.
Book design by Amelia Hoare

Published by Regina Press.

Printed in Hong Kong.
All rights reserved.

ISBN: 088 271 6476

A TREASURY OF CATHOLIC PRAYERS

THE REGINA PRESS · NEW YORK

I have a mission...

I am a link in a chain,

a bond of connection between persons.

God has not created me for naught...

Therefore I will trust him.

Whatever, wherever I am,

I can never be thrown away.

God does nothing in vain.

He knows what he is about.

J.H. Newman

CONTENTS

PRAISE GOD

Praise the LORD!
Praise him with trumpet sound;
  praise him with lute and harp!
Let everything that breathes
  praise the LORD!

Psalm 150

9

Bless the Lord, you angels of the Lord;
sing praise to him and highly
exalt him forever.

Daniel 3, 59

Praise be my Lord God,
and all God's creatures,
especially our brother, the sun,
who brings us the day
and who brings us the light;
fair is the sun, shining with great splendor.
O Lord, the sun is a sign to us of you.
Praise be my Lord, for our sister the moon,
and for the stars, set clear and lovely
in the heavens.
Praise be my Lord, for our brother the wind,
for air and clouds, and all good weather
that sustains life and all living creatures.
Praise be my Lord, for our mother the earth,
who sustains and keeps us,
and brings forth so many fruits
and many colored flowers
and plants.
Praise and bless the Lord,
giving thanks and serving the Lord humbly.

Canticle of the Sun, St. Francis of Assisi (1181-1226)

Hail Mary, full of grace,
the Lord is with you.
Blessed are you among women,
and blessed is the fruit of your womb, Jesus.
Holy Mary, Mother of God,
pray for us sinners,
now and at the hour of our death.
Amen.

Trinitatis nobile Triclinium

Hear my cry, O God;
listen to my prayer.
For you, O God, have heard my vows.

Psalm 61

Why are you cast down, O my soul,
and why are you disquieted
within me?
Hope in God; for I shall again
praise him,
my help and my God

Psalm 42

I thank you, Lord Jesus Christ,
for all you have given to us,
for all the pains and insults you bore for us
O most merciful Redeemer,
friend and brother,
may we know you more clearly,
love you more dearly,
and follow you more nearly.

St. Richard of Chichester (1197-1253)

COME, FOLLOW ME

Have mercy on me, O God,
according to your steadfast love;
according to your abundant mercy
blot out my transgressions.
Wash me thoroughly from my iniquity,
and cleanse me from my sin.
Create on me a clean heart, O God,
and put a new and right spirit within me.
Restore to me the joy of your salvation, and
sustain in me a willing spirit.
O Lord, open my lips,
and my mouth will declare your praise.
Do good to Zion in your good pleasure;
rebuild the walls of Jerusalem.

Psalm 51

After he had washed their feet, had put on his robe, and had returned to the table, he said to them, "Do you know what I have done to you? You call me Teacher and Lord—and you are right, for that is what I am. So if I, your Lord and Teacher, have washed your feet, you also ought to wash one another's feet. For I have set you an example, that you also should do as I have done."

John 13, 12-15

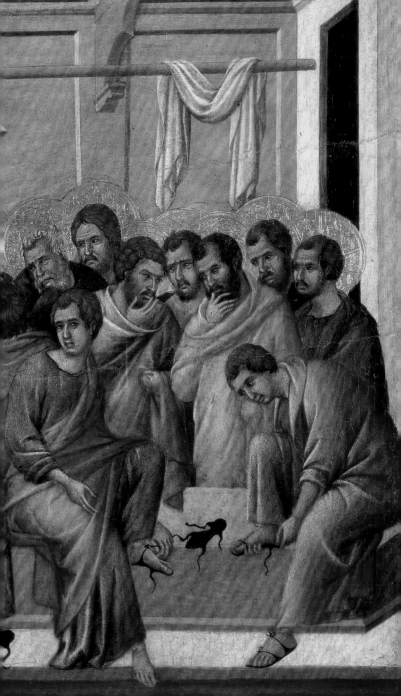

So I was taught that love is our Lord's meaning. And I saw surely in this and in all, that before God made us he loved us, which love was never slaked and never shall be.

Julian of Norwich

For the same reason you also pay taxes, for the authorities are God's servants, busy with this very thing. Pay to all what is due them - taxes to whom taxes are due, revenue to whom revenue is due, respect to whom respect is due, honor to whom honor is due.

Romans 13, 6-7

25

KNOWING the LORD

Lord Jesus Christ,
your blessing is for us all.
You manifested a new birth to the world,
a new patience in your Passion,
a new power in your Resurrection.
Send your Spirit and we shall be created
and you shall renew the face of the earth.

Ancient Collect

O God, may all I do today
be inspired by you
and continue with your saving help.
Let my work always begin with your blessing
and through you reach completion.

Roman Missal

The LORD will keep you from all evil;
he will keep your life. The LORD will keep
your going out and your coming in from
this time on and for evermore.   *Psalm 121*

O God, in you we live and move and have our being. Guide us by your Holy Spirit, so that in our cares and occupations, we may not forget you, but remember we are ever walking in your sight. Amen.

Ancient Collect

I am busy, O Lord, today.
If I forget you, do not forget me.

FAMILY AND FRIENDS

O God,
bless our family
and all its members and friends;
bind us together by your love.
Give us kindness and patience
to support each other;
and wisdom in all we do.
Let the gift of your peace
come into our hearts
and remain with us.
May we rejoice in your blessings
for all our day.
Amen.

O God, whose mighty Son was born in Bethlehem long ago, lead us to that same poor place, where Mary laid her tiny Child. And as we look in wonder and praise, help us welcome him an all new life, see him in the poor, and care for his handiwork, the earth, the sky and the sea. O God bless us again in your great love. Amen.

This is my commandment, that you love one another as I have loved you. I am giving you these commands so that you may love one another.

John 15, 12, 17

Where charity and love prevail,
there God is ever found.
Brought here by Christ's love,
by love are we thus bound.

Forgive we now each other's faults,
as we our faults confess.
And let us love each other well,
in Christian holiness.

Ancient Holy Thursday Hymn

THE NEEDS
OF THE WORLD

Lord, make me an instrument of
Your peace.
Where there is hatred, let me sow love;
Where there is injury, pardon;
Where there is doubt, faith;
Where there is despair, hope;
Where there is darkness, light;
And where there is sadness, joy.

O Divine Master,
Grant that I may not so much seek
To be consoled as to console;
To be understood as to understand;
To be loved as to love;
For it is in giving that we receive;
It is in pardoning that we are pardoned;
And it is in dying that we are born to
eternal life.

St. Francis of Assisi (1181-1226)

One day Peter and John were going up to the temple at the hour of prayer, at three o'clock in the afternoon. And a man lame from birth was being carried in. People would lay him daily at the gate of the temple called the Beautiful Gate so he could ask for alms from those entering the temple. When he saw Peter and John about to go into the temple, he asked them for alms.

Acts 3, 1-3

Then he sent them to Bethlehem, saying, "Go and search diligently for the child; and when you have found him, bring me word so that I may also go and pay him homage." When they had heard the king, they set out; and there ahead of them, went the star that they had seen at its rising, until it stopped over the place where the child was. Then they saw that the star had stopped, they were overwhelmed with joy. On entering the house, they saw the child with Mary his Mother; and they knelt down and paid him homage. Then, opening their treasure chests, they offered him gifts of gold, frankincense, and myrrh.

Matthew 2, 8-11

"Every creature is a word of God and a book about God."

Meister Eckhart

O God, you love our earth.
From sunrise to sunset
you fill land and sea
with riches;
the hills rejoice at your touch;
the valleys shout for joy,
Yes, they sing.

Your resplendent world
enables us to see you.
May we, made in your image,
care for the earth with love
all our days,
so that its pure song
of air, water and trees
broaden our minds
and lift up our hearts.
Amen.

IN TIME OF TROUBLE

Blessed be the God and Father of our Lord Jesus Christ, the Father of mercies and the God of all consolation, who consoles us in all our affliction, so that we may be able to console those who are in any affliction with the consolation with which we ourselves are consoled by God. For just as the sufferings of Christ are abundant for us, so also our consolation and salvation; if we are being consoled, it is for your consolation, which you experience when you patiently endure the same sufferings that we are also suffering. Our hope for you is unshaken; for we know that as you share in our sufferings, so also you share in our consolation.

2 Corinthians 1, 3-7

Once you guided Noah over the flood waves: hear us.

Once you called Jonah from the deep: deliver us.

Once you stretched your hand to Peter as he sank: help us, O Lord.

Son of God, who once did marvelous things, hear and help us now.

Adapted from an ancient Scottish Prayer

The poor are the church's treasure.

St. Lawrence the Deacon

We beg you, Lord,
to help and defend us.

Deliver the oppressed.
Pity the insignificant.
Raise the fallen.
Show yourself to the needy.
Heal the sick.
Bring back those of your people
who have gone astray.
Feed the hungry.
Lift up the weak.
Take off the prisoners' chains.

May every nation come to know
that Jesus is your child,
that we are your people,
the sheep that you pasture.
Amen. *St. Clement of Rome*

Then Jesus said to him, "What do you want me to do for you?" The blind man said to him, "My teacher, let me see again." Jesus said to him, "Go; your faith has made you well." Immediately he regained his sight and followed him on the way.

Mark 10, 51-52

May we grow in grace,
and in the knowledge
of our Lord and Savior,
season after season,
year after year,
till he takes to himself,
first one, the another,
in the order he thinks fit,
to be separated from each other
for a little while,
to be united together for ever,
in the kingdom of his Father
and our Father,
his God and our God.

Cardinal Newman

I am going to send an angel in front of you, to guard you on the way and bring you to the place that I have prepared. Be attentive to him and listen to his voice; do not rebel against him, for he will not pardon your transgression; for my name is in him.

But if you listen attentively to his voice and do all that I say, then I will be an enemy to your enemies and a foe to your foes.

Exodus 23, 20-22

PRAYERS
FOR EVERY DAY

Our Father, who art in heaven,
hallowed be thy name;
thy kingdom come;
thy will be done on earth as it is in heaven.
Give us this day our daily bread;
and forgive us our trespasses
as we forgive those trespass against us;
and lead us not into temptation,
but deliver us from evil. Amen.

St. Michael, the Archangel,
defend us in battle.

Rejoice in the Lord, always; again I will say, Rejoice. Let your gentleness be known to everyone. The Lord is near.

Do not worry about anything, but in everything by prayer and supplication with thanksgiving let your requests be made known to God.

Philippians 4, 4-6

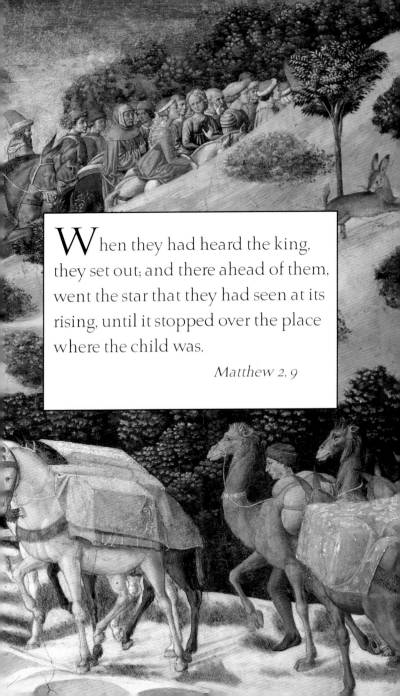

W hen they had heard the king,
they set out; and there ahead of them,
went the star that they had seen at its
rising, until it stopped over the place
where the child was.

Matthew 2, 9

God be in my head,
and in my understanding;
God be in my eyes,
and in my looking;
God be in my mouth,
and in my speaking;
God be in my heart,
and in my thinking;
God be at my end,
and at my departing.

16th century Sarum Primer

64

Let us fix our eyes on Jesus,
the author and perfecter of our faith,
who for the joy set before him endured
the cross, scorning shame, and sat down
at the right hand of the throne of God.

Hebrews 12, 2

Tell us, Mary, what did you see
that early morning, on your way?
"I saw his tomb, I saw the glory of Christ,
now risen, angels who gave witness. I saw
the clothes that covered his head and
body. And I heard him speak my name."

Adapted from an Ancient Easter Hymn

He said to them, "Why are you fright-
ened, and why do doubts arise in your
hearts? Look at my hands and feet:
see that it is I myself."

Luke 24, 38-39

Then he looked up at his disciples
and said:
Blessed are you who are poor,
for yours is the kingdom of God.
Blessed are you who are hungry now,
for you will be filled.
Blessed are you who weep now,
for you will laugh.
Blessed are you when people hate you,
and when they exclude you,
revile you, and defame on account
of the Son of Man.
Rejoice in that day and leap for joy,
for surely your reward is great in heaven;
for that is what their ancestors
did to the prophets.

Luke 6, 20-23

Then Jesus came from Galilee to John at the Jordan, to be baptized by him. John would have prevented him, saying, "I need to be baptized by you, and do you come to me?" But Jesus answered him, "Let it be so now; for it is proper for us in this way to fulfill all righteousness." Then he consented. And when Jesus had been baptized, just as he came up from the water, suddenly the heavens were opened to him and he saw the Spirit of God descending like a dove and alighting on him. And a voice from heaven said, "This is my Son, the Beloved, with whom I am well pleased."

Psalm 150

Teach us, good Lord, to serve you
as you deserve:
to give and not count the cost;
to fight and not heed the wounds;
to toil and not ask for rest;
to labor and not ask for any reward
except that of knowing that we do your will.

St. Ignatius of Loyola (1491-1556)

Bless us, O Lord, and these your gifts
which we have received
through Christ our Lord.
Amen.

Lord, bless our meal
and as you satisfy our needs,
make us mindful of the needs of others.
Amen.

May the Lord bless us and keep us;
May the Lord let his face shine upon us;
May the Lord look upon us kindly
and give us peace.
Amen.

God in heaven, bless the food of earth and bless us at this table with every gift from above.

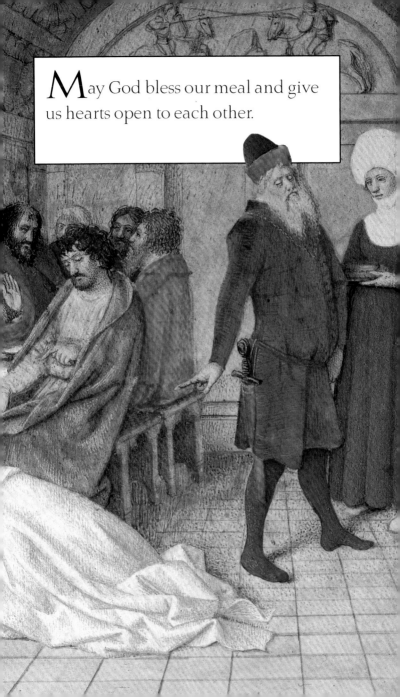

May God bless our meal and give us hearts open to each other.

FAMILY PRAYER.

God made us a family.

We need one another; we love one another.

We forgive one another; we work together.

We play together; we worship together.

Together we use God's word. Together we grow in Christ. Together we love all men.

Together we serve our God.

Together we hope for Heaven.

These are our hopes and ideals.

Help us to attain them, O God,

through Jesus Christ, our Lord.

Then Mary said, "Here am I, the servant of the Lord; let it be with me according to your word." Then the angel departed from her.   *Luke 1, 38*

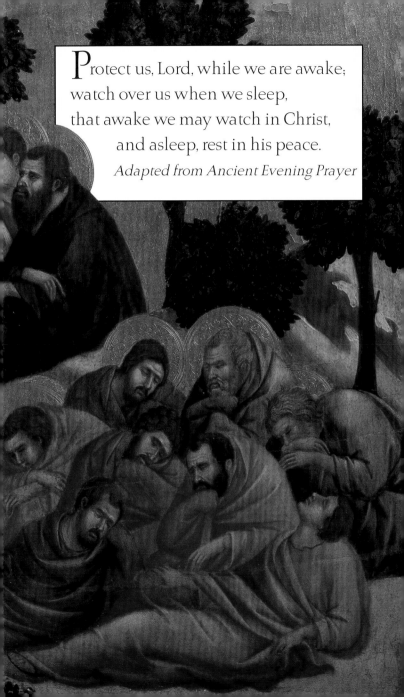

Protect us, Lord, while we are awake;
watch over us when we sleep,
that awake we may watch in Christ,
and asleep, rest in his peace.

Adapted from Ancient Evening Prayer

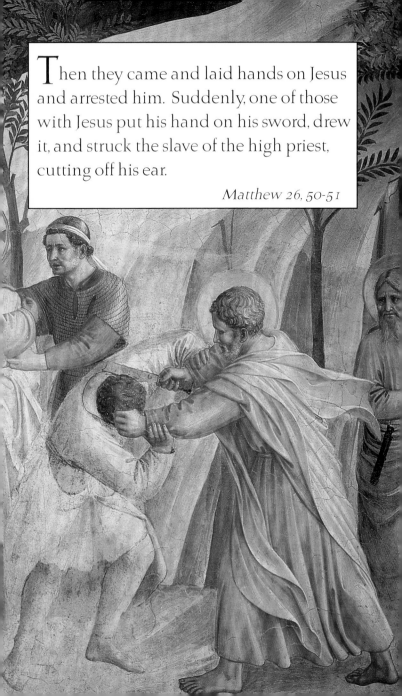

Then they came and laid hands on Jesus and arrested him. Suddenly, one of those with Jesus put his hand on his sword, drew it, and struck the slave of the high priest, cutting off his ear.

Matthew 26, 50-51

Great and amazing are your deeds,
Lord God the Almighty!
Just and true are your ways,
King of the nations!
Lord, who will not fear
and glorify your name?
For you alone are holy.
All nations will come
and worship before you,
for your judgements have been revealed.

Revelations 15, 3-4

INDEX OF ARTISTS AND PAINTINGS

PAGE 6
The Coronation of the Virgin
(detail)
The San Pier Maggiore
Altarpiece
Attrib. JACOPO DI CIONE
(active c. 1449; died 1398/1400)
The National Gallery, London

FRONT AND BACK
ENDPAPERS
Journey of the Magi
(detail) Fresco
BENOZZO GOZZOLI
(c. 1421-1497)
*Palazzo Medici-Riccardi,
Florence*

PAGE 5
The Madonna and Child
(detail)
WILLIAM DYCE
(1806-1864)
Osborne House, Isle of Wight

PAGE 8
A Choir of Angels *(detail)*
SIMON MARMION
(active 1449; died 1489)
The National Gallery, London

PAGE 9
Coronation of the Virgin
Panel of a Polyptych
Workshop of
GIOTTO DI BONDONE
(c. 1266-1337)
*Baroncelli Chapel, Church of
Santa Croce, Florence*

PAGE 12
Saint Francis Preaching
to the Birds *(detail)*
GIOTTO DI BONDONE
(c. 1266-1337)
*S. Francis, Upper Church,
Assisi*

PAGES 10-11
Journey of the Magi
(detail) Fresco
BENOZZO GOZZOLI
(c. 1421-1497)
*Palazzo Medici-Riccardi,
Florence*

PAGES 14-15
The Annunciation (detail) Fresco
FRA ANGELICO (c. 1395-1455)
Museo di S. Marco, Florence

PAGE 16
The Young Cicero Reading (detail) Fresco
VINCENZO FOPPA (active 1456-c. 1515)
Wallace Collection, London

PAGE 17
Portrait of an Old Man
(detail)
FILIPPINO LIPPI
(c. 1457-1504)
Galleria degli Uffizi,
Florence

PAGE 18
The Dead Christ
supported by Two Angels
(detail)
CARLO CRIVELLI
(c. 1430/5-c. 1494)
The National Gallery, London

PAGE 19
Mary Magdalen
(detail)
The Braque Family Triptych
ROGIER VAN DER WEYDEN
(c. 1399-1464)
Louvre, Paris

PAGE 20
Adam and Eve
banished from Paradise
(detail)
RAMON DE MURE
(active 1412-1435)
Museu Espiscopal,
Vic

PAGES 22-23
Christ Washing
the Disciples' Feet
(detail)
DUCCIO DI BUONINSEGNA
(active 1278-c.1319)
Museo dell'Opera
del Duomo, Siena

PAGE 24
Christ in the House of
Martha and Mary
(detail)
JAN VERMEER
(1632-1675)
National Gallery of Scotland,
Edinburgh

PAGE 25
The Tribute Money
TITIAN
(active c. 1506; died 1576)
*The National Gallery,
London*

PAGE 26
Saint Jerome in his Study
(detail)
DOMINICO GHIRLANDAIO
(1449-1494)
Galleria degli Uffizi, Florence

PAGE 27
Crucifixion (detail)
PIETRO PERUGINO
(living 1469; died 1523)
*Church of S. Agostino,
Siena*

PAGE 28
A Girl Writing
(detail)
NETHERLANDISH SCHOOL
(c. 1520)
*The National Gallery,
London*

PAGE 29
St. Christopher
MASTER OF THE
EMBROIDERED FOLIAGE
(active c. 1500)
*Gemäldegalerie
Alte Meister, Dresden*

PAGE 30-31
Saint Eloi in the Silversmith's
Workshop (detail)
TADDEO GADDI (c. 1300-
1366)
Prado, Madrid

PAGES 32
The Scullery Maid
(detail)
GIUSEPPE MARIA CRESPI
(1665-1747)
*Fondazione
Contini Bonacossi,
Florence*

PAGE 33
Saint Joseph, the Carpenter (detail)
GEORGES DE LA TOUR (1593-1652)
Louvre, Paris

PAGE 34
The Holy Family with
Saints Elizabeth
and John *(detail)*
After NICHOLAS POUSSIN
(after 1640)
*The National Gallery,
London*

PAGES 36-38
'Mystic Nativity' *(details)*
SANDRO BOTTICELLI (c. 1445-1510)
The National Gallery, London

PAGE 40
The Conversion of
Saint Hubert *(detail)*
Workshop of the
MASTER OF THE LIFE
OF THE VIRGIN
(c. 1480/85)
The National Gallery,
London

PAGES 42-43
Saint Peter Healing a Cripple *(detail)* Fresco
MASOLINO (c. 1383-after 1432)
*Brancacci Chapel, Santa Maria del Carmine,
Florence*

PAGE 44
The
Adoration of the Magi
(detail)
HUGO VAN DER GOES
(active 1467; died 1482)
Hermitage, St. Petersburg

PAGE 47
Saint Giles and the Hind
(detail)
MASTER OF SAINT GILES,
(active c. 1500)
*The National Gallery,
London*

PAGE 48
Saint John leading home
his Adopted Mother
(detail)
WILLIAM DYCE (1806-1864)
*Forbes Magazine Collection,
London*

PAGES 50-51
Miraculous Draught of Fishes
(detail)
KONRAD WITZ (1400/10-1444/6)
Musee d'Art et d'Histoire, Geneva

PAGE 52
Saint Lawrence
distributing alms (detail)
FRA ANGELICO (c. 1395-1455)
Chapel of Nicholas V,
Vatican, Rome

PAGE 54
The Blind of Jericho, or Christ
Healing the Blind (detail)
NICHOLAS POUSSIN (1594-1665)
Louvre, Paris

PAGE 55
Seven Saints
FRA FILIPPO LIPPO (C. 1406-1469)
The National Gallery, London

PAGE 57
Tobias and the Angel
(detail)
Attrib. ANDREA DEL VERROCCHIO
(C. 1435-1488)
The National Gallery, London

PAGE 58
Agony in the Garden
(detail)
SANDRO BOTTICELLI
(c. 1445-1510)
Capilla Real, Granada

PAGE 60
Saint Michael (detail)
BERNADINO ZENALE
(1436-1526)
Galleria degli Uffizi,
France

FRONT JACKET AND PAGE 61
Saint Catherine (detail)
After BERNARDINO LUINI
(active 1512; died 1532)
The National Gallery, London

PAGES 62-63
Journey of the Magi
(detail) Fresco
BENOZZO GOZZOLI
(c. 1421-1497)
Palazzo Medici-Riccardi,
Florence

PAGE 64
Head of a Saint (detail)
VENEZIANO DOMENICO
(active 1438; died 1461)
The National Gallery,
London

PAGE 65
The Trinity (detail)
J. BACO (1410-1461) and
J. REXACH (1415-1484)
Musee de Picardie, Amiens

PAGE 66
Noli me tangere
FRA ANGELICO
(c. 1395-1455)
Museo di S. Marco,
Florence

PAGE 67
Resurrection (detail)
PIERO DELLA FRANCESCA
(1410/20-1492)
Pinacoteca Comunale,
Sansepolcro

PAGE 69
The Charity of
Saint Lucy (detail)
JACOBELLO DEL FIORE
(died 1439)
Pinacoteca Civica, Fermo

PAGE 70
Baptism of Christ
(detail)
Workshop of
BICCI DI LORENZO (1375-1452)
York City Art Gallery

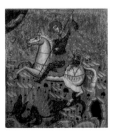

PAGE 71
Saint George and
the Dragon (detail) Icon
SYRIAN
Early Period (c. 800)

PAGE 73
The Marriage Feast
at Cana (detail)
JUAN DE FLANDRES
(active from 1496;
died before 1519)
Private Collection

PAGE 74-75
Mary Magdalen
washing Christ's feet
(detail)
The Hours of Eteinne Chevalier
JEAN FOUQUET (c. 1425-1480)
Musee Conde, Chantilly

PAGE 76
Holy Family with
a Palm Tree
Tondo
RAPHAEL (1483-1520)
Duke of Sutherland
Collection, on loan to
the National Gallery of Scotland,
Edinburgh

PAGE 77
The Annunciation
(detail)
Panel from
the Main Altarpiece
JUAN DE FLANDRES
(active from 1496;
died before 1519)
Palencia Cathdral,
Palencia

PAGES 78-79
Agony in the Garden
of Gethsemene
(detail)
DUCCIO DI BUONINSEGNA
(active 1278-C. 1319)
Museo dell'Opera
del Duomo, Siena

PAGES 80-81
The Arrest of Jesus (detail)
FRA ANGELICO (C. 1395-1455)
Museo di San Marco
dell'Angelico, Florence

PAGE 82
God the Father Enthroned
(detail)
Polyptych of the Apocalypse
JACOPO ALBEREGNO
(died 1397)
Galleria dell'Accademia,
Venice

BACK JACKET
The Virgin in a Rose Arbour (detail)
STEPHAN LOCHNER (active 1442-1451)
Wallraf-Richartz Museum, Cologne

PHOTOGRAPHIC ACKNOWLEDGEMENTS

For permission to reproduce the paintings on the following pages and for supplying photographs, the Publishers thank:

Bridgeman Art Library, London: Endpapers, 9, 10-11, 12, 16, 17, 19, 20, 22-23, 24, 26, 27, 30-31, 42-43, 44, 48, 50-51, 52, 58, 60, 62-63, 69, 70, 74-75, 76, 78-79, 80-81, 82, back jacket

Christie's London/Bridgeman Art Library, London: 73

Gemäldegalerie Alte Meister, Dresden: 29

Giraudon/Bridgeman Art Library, London: 33, 54, 65

Index/Bridgeman Art Library, London: 77

The National Gallery, London: front jacket, 6, 8, 18, 25, 28, 34, 36-37, 38, 40, 47, 55, 57, 61, 64

Richardson and Kailas Icons, London/Bridgeman Art Library, London: 71

The Royal Collection © 1996 Her Majesty Queen Elizabeth II: 5

Scala, Florence: 14-15, 32, 66, 67

PRAYERS

Sign of the Cross

In the name of the Father,
    and of the Son, ✝ and of the
    Holy Spirit.
    Amen.

The Lord's Prayer

Our Father, who art in heaven,
    hallowed be thy name;
    thy kingdom come;
    thy will be done on earth as it is
    in heaven.

Give us this day our daily bread;
    and forgive us our trespasses
    as we forgive those who trespass
    against us;
    and lead us not into temptation,
    but deliver us from evil.
    Amen.

The Hail Mary

Hail Mary, full of grace,
    the Lord is with you.
    Blessed are you among women,
    and blessed is the fruit
    of your womb, Jesus.

Holy Mary, Mother of God,
    pray for us sinners,
    now and at the hour of our death.
    Amen.

Glory Be to the Father

Glory be to the Father, and to the Son, and
to the Holy Spirit.
As it was in the beginning, is now and
ever shall be, world without end. Amen.

The Apostles' Creed

I believe in God, the Father almighty,
Creator of heaven and earth.

I believe in Jesus Christ, his only Son, our
Lord. He was conceived by the power of
the Holy Spirit
and born of the Virgin Mary.
He suffered under Pontius Pilate, was
crucified, died and was buried. He
descended to the dead.
On the third day he rose again.
He ascended into heaven,
and is seated at the right hand
of the Father.
He will come again to judge
the living and the dead.

I believe in the Holy Spirit,
the holy catholic Church,
the communion of saints,
the forgiveness of sins,
the resurrection of the body,
and life everlasting.
Amen.